NOTEBOOK

PERSONAL DETAILS

Name : _____

Address : _____

Email : _____

Phone Number : _____

Fax Number : _____

Log Start Date : _____

Log Book Number : _____

ADDITIONAL INFORMATION

Date	Client Name	Contact No	Session No	Page#	Notes
Date	Client Name	Contact No	Session No	Page#	Notes

Date	Client Name	Contact No	Session No	Page#	Notes

Date	Client Name	Contact No	Session No	Page#	Notes

Date: _____ Start time: _____ Session No: _____
Client Name: _____ Topic: _____

Session Talking Points:　　　　　　　　　Key Points from Previous Session:
✓ _____　　✓ _____
✓ _____　　✓ _____
✓ _____　　✓ _____
✓ _____　　✓ _____

Notes:

Extra Notes :

Client Actions :

- ✓
- ✓
- ✓
- ✓
- ✓
- ✓

Concerns :

- ✓
- ✓
- ✓

Recommendations :

- ✓
- ✓
- ✓

Overall Comments :

Next Session Talking Points :

- ✓
- ✓
- ✓
- ✓
- ✓
- ✓

Next Session Date : _____   End Time : _____

Date: _____ Start time: _____ Session No: _____
Client Name: _____ Topic: _____

Session Talking Points:
- ✓ _____
- ✓ _____
- ✓ _____
- ✓ _____

Key Points from Previous Session:
- ✓ _____
- ✓ _____
- ✓ _____
- ✓ _____

Notes: _____

Extra Notes :

Client Actions :

- ✓
- ✓
- ✓

- ✓
- ✓
- ✓

Concerns :

- ✓
- ✓
- ✓

Recommendations :

- ✓
- ✓
- ✓

Overall Comments :

Next Session Talking Points :

- ✓
- ✓
- ✓

- ✓
- ✓
- ✓

Next Session Date : _____   End Time : _____

Date: Start time: Session No:

Client Name: Topic:

Session Talking Points:
- ✓
- ✓
- ✓
- ✓

Key Points from Previous Session:
- ✓
- ✓
- ✓
- ✓

Notes:

Extra Notes :

Client Actions :

- ✓
- ✓
- ✓
- ✓
- ✓
- ✓

Concerns :

- ✓
- ✓
- ✓

Recommendations :

- ✓
- ✓
- ✓

Overall Comments :

Next Session Talking Points :

- ✓
- ✓
- ✓
- ✓
- ✓
- ✓

Next Session Date :   End Time :

Date :   Start time :   Session No :

Client Name :   Topic :

Session Talking Points :
- ✓
- ✓
- ✓
- ✓

Key Points from Previous Session :
- ✓
- ✓
- ✓
- ✓

Notes :

Extra Notes :

Client Actions :

- ✓
- ✓
- ✓

- ✓
- ✓
- ✓

Concerns :

- ✓
- ✓
- ✓

Recommendations :

- ✓
- ✓
- ✓

Overall Comments :

Next Session Talking Points :

- ✓
- ✓
- ✓

- ✓
- ✓
- ✓

Next Session Date :   End Time :

Date :   Start time :   Session No :

Client Name :   Topic :

Session Talking Points :
- ✓
- ✓
- ✓
- ✓

Key Points from Previous Session :
- ✓
- ✓
- ✓
- ✓

Notes :

Extra Notes :

___

Client Actions :

- ✓
- ✓
- ✓

- ✓
- ✓
- ✓

Concerns :

- ✓
- ✓
- ✓

Recommendations :

- ✓
- ✓
- ✓

Overall Comments :

___

Next Session Talking Points :

- ✓
- ✓
- ✓

- ✓
- ✓
- ✓

Next Session Date : _____   End Time : _____

Date : _____ Start time : _____ Session No : _____
Client Name : _____ Topic : _____

Session Talking Points :   Key Points from Previous Session :
✓ _____   ✓ _____
✓ _____   ✓ _____
✓ _____   ✓ _____
✓ _____   ✓ _____

Notes : _____

Extra Notes :

Client Actions :

- ✓
- ✓
- ✓

- ✓
- ✓
- ✓

Concerns :

- ✓
- ✓
- ✓

Recommendations :

- ✓
- ✓
- ✓

Overall Comments :

Next Session Talking Points :

- ✓
- ✓
- ✓

- ✓
- ✓
- ✓

Next Session Date :   End Time :

Date :   Start time :   Session No :

Client Name :   Topic :

Session Talking Points :
-
-
-
-

Key Points from Previous Session :
-
-
-
-

Notes :

Extra Notes :

Client Actions :

- ✓
- ✓
- ✓

- ✓
- ✓
- ✓

Concerns :

- ✓
- ✓
- ✓

Recommendations :

- ✓
- ✓
- ✓

Overall Comments :

Next Session Talking Points :

- ✓
- ✓
- ✓

- ✓
- ✓
- ✓

Next Session Date :   End Time :

Date :   Start time :   Session No :

Client Name :   Topic :

Session Talking Points :
- ✓
- ✓
- ✓
- ✓

Key Points from Previous Session :
- ✓
- ✓
- ✓
- ✓

Notes :

Extra Notes :

Client Actions :

- ✓
- ✓
- ✓

Concerns :

- ✓
- ✓
- ✓

Recommendations :

- ✓
- ✓
- ✓

Overall Comments :

Next Session Talking Points :

- ✓
- ✓
- ✓

Next Session Date : _____ End Time : _____

Date :   Start time :   Session No :

Client Name :   Topic :

Session Talking Points :   Key Points from Previous Session :

- ✓
- ✓
- ✓
- ✓

- ✓
- ✓
- ✓
- ✓

Notes :

Extra Notes :

Client Actions :
- ✓
- ✓
- ✓

- ✓
- ✓
- ✓

Concerns :
- ✓
- ✓
- ✓

Recommendations :
- ✓
- ✓
- ✓

Overall Comments :

Next Session Talking Points :
- ✓
- ✓
- ✓

- ✓
- ✓
- ✓

Next Session Date : _____ End Time : _____

Date : _____ Start time : _____ Session No : _____
Client Name : _____ Topic : _____

Session Talking Points :   Key Points from Previous Session :
✓ _____   ✓ _____
✓ _____   ✓ _____
✓ _____   ✓ _____
✓ _____   ✓ _____

Notes :

Extra Notes :

Client Actions :

- ✓
- ✓
- ✓

✓
✓
✓

Concerns :

- ✓
- ✓
- ✓

Recommendations :

- ✓
- ✓
- ✓

Overall Comments :

Next Session Talking Points :

- ✓
- ✓
- ✓

✓
✓
✓

Next Session Date : _____   End Time : _____

Date: Start time: Session No:

Client Name: Topic:

Session Talking Points:
- ✓
- ✓
- ✓
- ✓

Key Points from Previous Session:
- ✓
- ✓
- ✓
- ✓

Notes:

Extra Notes :

Client Actions :
- ✓
- ✓
- ✓
- ✓
- ✓
- ✓

Concerns :
- ✓
- ✓
- ✓

Recommendations :
- ✓
- ✓
- ✓

Overall Comments :

Next Session Talking Points :
- ✓
- ✓
- ✓
- ✓
- ✓
- ✓

Next Session Date : _____   End Time : _____

Date :   Start time :   Session No :

Client Name :   Topic :

Session Talking Points :
- ✓
- ✓
- ✓
- ✓

Key Points from Previous Session :
- ✓
- ✓
- ✓
- ✓

Notes :

Extra Notes :

Client Actions :

- ✓
- ✓
- ✓

- ✓
- ✓
- ✓

Concerns :

- ✓
- ✓
- ✓

Recommendations :

- ✓
- ✓
- ✓

Overall Comments :

Next Session Talking Points :

- ✓
- ✓
- ✓

- ✓
- ✓
- ✓

Next Session Date : _____   End Time : _____

Date : _____ Start time : _____ Session No : _____
Client Name : _____ Topic : _____

Session Talking Points :
- ✓ _____
- ✓ _____
- ✓ _____
- ✓ _____

Key Points from Previous Session :
- ✓ _____
- ✓ _____
- ✓ _____
- ✓ _____

Notes : _____

Extra Notes :

Client Actions :

- ✓
- ✓
- ✓

- ✓
- ✓
- ✓

Concerns :

- ✓
- ✓
- ✓

Recommendations :

- ✓
- ✓
- ✓

Overall Comments :

Next Session Talking Points :

- ✓
- ✓
- ✓

- ✓
- ✓
- ✓

Next Session Date : _____ End Time : _____

Date : _____ Start time : _____ Session No : _____
Client Name : _____ Topic : _____

Session Talking Points :	Key Points from Previous Session :
✓ _____	✓ _____
✓ _____	✓ _____
✓ _____	✓ _____
✓ _____	✓ _____

Notes :

Extra Notes :

Client Actions :

- ✓
- ✓
- ✓

✓
✓
✓

Concerns :

- ✓
- ✓
- ✓

Recommendations :

✓
✓
✓

Overall Comments :

Next Session Talking Points :

- ✓
- ✓
- ✓

✓
✓
✓

Next Session Date : _____   End Time : _____

Date :   Start time :   Session No :

Client Name :   Topic :

Session Talking Points :
- ✓
- ✓
- ✓
- ✓

Key Points from Previous Session :
- ✓
- ✓
- ✓
- ✓

Notes :

Extra Notes :

Client Actions :

- ✓
- ✓
- ✓

- ✓
- ✓
- ✓

Concerns :

- ✓
- ✓
- ✓

Recommendations :

- ✓
- ✓
- ✓

Overall Comments :

Next Session Talking Points :

- ✓
- ✓
- ✓

- ✓
- ✓
- ✓

Next Session Date : _____   End Time : _____

Date : _____ Start time : _____ Session No : _____
Client Name : _____ Topic : _____

Session Talking Points :
- ✓ _____
- ✓ _____
- ✓ _____
- ✓ _____

Key Points from Previous Session :
- ✓ _____
- ✓ _____
- ✓ _____
- ✓ _____

Notes :

Extra Notes :

Client Actions :

- ✓
- ✓
- ✓

- ✓
- ✓
- ✓

Concerns :

- ✓
- ✓
- ✓

Recommendations :

- ✓
- ✓
- ✓

Overall Comments :

Next Session Talking Points :

- ✓
- ✓
- ✓

- ✓
- ✓
- ✓

Next Session Date : _____ End Time : _____

Date: Start time: Session No:
Client Name: Topic:

Session Talking Points:
- ✓
- ✓
- ✓
- ✓

Key Points from Previous Session:
- ✓
- ✓
- ✓
- ✓

Notes:

Extra Notes :

Client Actions :

- ✓
- ✓
- ✓

✓
✓
✓

Concerns :

Recommendations :

- ✓
- ✓
- ✓

✓
✓
✓

Overall Comments :

Next Session Talking Points :

- ✓
- ✓
- ✓

✓
✓
✓

Next Session Date : _____ End Time : _____

Date : _____   Start time : _____   Session No : _____
Client Name : _____   Topic : _____

Session Talking Points :
- ✓ _____
- ✓ _____
- ✓ _____
- ✓ _____

Key Points from Previous Session :
- ✓ _____
- ✓ _____
- ✓ _____
- ✓ _____

Notes : _____

Extra Notes :

Client Actions :

- ✓
- ✓
- ✓

✓
✓
✓

Concerns :

- ✓
- ✓
- ✓

Recommendations :

- ✓
- ✓
- ✓

Overall Comments :

Next Session Talking Points :

- ✓
- ✓
- ✓

✓
✓
✓

Next Session Date : _____   End Time : _____

Date : _____ Start time : _____ Session No : _____
Client Name : _____ Topic : _____

Session Talking Points :   Key Points from Previous Session :
✓ _____   ✓ _____
✓ _____   ✓ _____
✓ _____   ✓ _____
✓ _____   ✓ _____

Notes :

Extra Notes :

Client Actions :

- ✓
- ✓
- ✓
- ✓
- ✓
- ✓

Concerns :

- ✓
- ✓
- ✓

Recommendations :

- ✓
- ✓
- ✓

Overall Comments :

Next Session Talking Points :

- ✓
- ✓
- ✓
- ✓
- ✓
- ✓

Next Session Date :   End Time :

Date : Start time : Session No :

Client Name : Topic :

Session Talking Points :   Key Points from Previous Session :
- ✓
- ✓
- ✓
- ✓

- ✓
- ✓
- ✓
- ✓

Notes :

Extra Notes :

Client Actions :

- ✓
- ✓
- ✓
- ✓
- ✓
- ✓

Concerns :

- ✓
- ✓
- ✓

Recommendations :

- ✓
- ✓
- ✓

Overall Comments :

Next Session Talking Points :

- ✓
- ✓
- ✓
- ✓
- ✓
- ✓

Next Session Date :   End Time :

Date : Start time : Session No :
Client Name : Topic :

Session Talking Points : Key Points from Previous Session :
- ✓
- ✓
- ✓
- ✓

- ✓
- ✓
- ✓
- ✓

Notes :

Extra Notes :

Client Actions :

-
-
-
-
-
-

Concerns :

-
-
-

Recommendations :

-
-
-

Overall Comments :

Next Session Talking Points :

-
-
-
-
-
-

Next Session Date :   End Time :

Date : _____ Start time : _____ Session No : _____
Client Name : _____ Topic : _____

Session Talking Points :   Key Points from Previous Session :
- ✓ _____   ✓ _____
- ✓ _____   ✓ _____
- ✓ _____   ✓ _____
- ✓ _____   ✓ _____

Notes : _____

_____
_____
_____
_____
_____
_____
_____
_____
_____
_____
_____
_____
_____
_____
_____
_____
_____
_____

Extra Notes :

Client Actions :

- ✓
- ✓
- ✓

- ✓
- ✓
- ✓

Concerns :

- ✓
- ✓
- ✓

Recommendations :

- ✓
- ✓
- ✓

Overall Comments :

Next Session Talking Points :

- ✓
- ✓
- ✓

- ✓
- ✓
- ✓

Next Session Date : _____   End Time : _____

Date :   Start time :   Session No :

Client Name :   Topic :

Session Talking Points :
- ✓
- ✓
- ✓
- ✓

Key Points from Previous Session :
- ✓
- ✓
- ✓
- ✓

Notes :

Extra Notes :

Client Actions :

- ✓
- ✓
- ✓

- ✓
- ✓
- ✓

Concerns :

- ✓
- ✓
- ✓

Recommendations :

- ✓
- ✓
- ✓

Overall Comments :

Next Session Talking Points :

- ✓
- ✓
- ✓

- ✓
- ✓
- ✓

Next Session Date :   End Time :

Date :   Start time :   Session No :

Client Name :   Topic :

Session Talking Points :
- ✓
- ✓
- ✓
- ✓

Key Points from Previous Session :
- ✓
- ✓
- ✓
- ✓

Notes :

Extra Notes :

Client Actions :

- ✓
- ✓
- ✓

- ✓
- ✓
- ✓

Concerns :

- ✓
- ✓
- ✓

Recommendations :

- ✓
- ✓
- ✓

Overall Comments :

Next Session Talking Points :

- ✓
- ✓
- ✓

- ✓
- ✓
- ✓

Next Session Date : _____ End Time : _____

Date : _____ Start time : _____ Session No : _____
Client Name : _____ Topic : _____

Session Talking Points :   Key Points from Previous Session :
✓ _____   ✓ _____
✓ _____   ✓ _____
✓ _____   ✓ _____
✓ _____   ✓ _____

Notes :

Extra Notes :

Client Actions :
- ✓
- ✓
- ✓
- ✓
- ✓
- ✓

Concerns :
- ✓
- ✓
- ✓

Recommendations :
- ✓
- ✓
- ✓

Overall Comments :

Next Session Talking Points :
- ✓
- ✓
- ✓
- ✓
- ✓
- ✓

Next Session Date : _____ End Time : _____

Date :   Start time :   Session No :

Client Name :   Topic :

Session Talking Points :
- ✓
- ✓
- ✓
- ✓

Key Points from Previous Session :
- ✓
- ✓
- ✓
- ✓

Notes :

Extra Notes :

Client Actions :

- ✓
- ✓
- ✓

- ✓
- ✓
- ✓

Concerns :

- ✓
- ✓
- ✓

Recommendations :

- ✓
- ✓
- ✓

Overall Comments :

Next Session Talking Points :

- ✓
- ✓
- ✓

- ✓
- ✓
- ✓

Next Session Date : _____ End Time : _____

Date : _____ Start time : _____ Session No : _____
Client Name : _____ Topic : _____

Session Talking Points :
- ✓ _____
- ✓ _____
- ✓ _____
- ✓ _____

Key Points from Previous Session :
- ✓ _____
- ✓ _____
- ✓ _____
- ✓ _____

Notes :

Extra Notes :

Client Actions :

- ✓
- ✓
- ✓

- ✓
- ✓
- ✓

Concerns :

- ✓
- ✓
- ✓

Recommendations :

- ✓
- ✓
- ✓

Overall Comments :

Next Session Talking Points :

- ✓
- ✓
- ✓

- ✓
- ✓
- ✓

Next Session Date : _____ End Time : _____

Date : _____ Start time : _____ Session No : _____
Client Name : _____ Topic : _____

Session Talking Points :
- ✓ _____
- ✓ _____
- ✓ _____
- ✓ _____

Key Points from Previous Session :
- ✓ _____
- ✓ _____
- ✓ _____
- ✓ _____

Notes :

Extra Notes :

Client Actions :

- ✓
- ✓
- ✓

- ✓
- ✓
- ✓

Concerns :

- ✓
- ✓
- ✓

Recommendations :

- ✓
- ✓
- ✓

Overall Comments :

Next Session Talking Points :

- ✓
- ✓
- ✓

- ✓
- ✓
- ✓

Next Session Date :   End Time :

Date : _____ Start time : _____ Session No : _____
Client Name : _____ Topic : _____

Session Talking Points :   Key Points from Previous Session :
✓ _____   ✓ _____
✓ _____   ✓ _____
✓ _____   ✓ _____
✓ _____   ✓ _____

Notes : _____

Extra Notes :

Client Actions :
- ✓
- ✓
- ✓
- ✓
- ✓
- ✓

Concerns :
- ✓
- ✓
- ✓

Recommendations :
- ✓
- ✓
- ✓

Overall Comments :

Next Session Talking Points :
- ✓
- ✓
- ✓
- ✓
- ✓
- ✓

Next Session Date :   End Time :

Date : Start time : Session No :

Client Name : Topic :

Session Talking Points :
- ✓
- ✓
- ✓
- ✓

Key Points from Previous Session :
- ✓
- ✓
- ✓
- ✓

Notes :

Extra Notes :

Client Actions :

-
-
-
-
-
-

Concerns :

-
-
-

Recommendations :

-
-
-

Overall Comments :

Next Session Talking Points :

-
-
-
-
-
-

Next Session Date :   End Time :

Date :   Start time :   Session No :

Client Name :   Topic :

Session Talking Points :   Key Points from Previous Session :

- ✓
- ✓
- ✓
- ✓

Notes :

Extra Notes :

Client Actions :

- ✓
- ✓
- ✓

- ✓
- ✓
- ✓

Concerns :

- ✓
- ✓
- ✓

Recommendations :

- ✓
- ✓
- ✓

Overall Comments :

Next Session Talking Points :

- ✓
- ✓
- ✓

- ✓
- ✓
- ✓

Next Session Date :   End Time :

Date :   Start time :   Session No :

Client Name :   Topic :

Session Talking Points :
- ✓
- ✓
- ✓
- ✓

Key Points from Previous Session :
- ✓
- ✓
- ✓
- ✓

Notes :

Extra Notes :

Client Actions :
- ✓
- ✓
- ✓
- ✓
- ✓
- ✓

Concerns :
- ✓
- ✓
- ✓

Recommendations :
- ✓
- ✓
- ✓

Overall Comments :

Next Session Talking Points :
- ✓
- ✓
- ✓
- ✓
- ✓
- ✓

Next Session Date :   End Time :

Date :   Start time :   Session No :

Client Name :   Topic :

Session Talking Points :
- ✓
- ✓
- ✓
- ✓

Key Points from Previous Session :
- ✓
- ✓
- ✓
- ✓

Notes :

Extra Notes :

Client Actions :

- ✓
- ✓
- ✓
- ✓
- ✓
- ✓

Concerns :

- ✓
- ✓
- ✓

Recommendations :

- ✓
- ✓
- ✓

Overall Comments :

Next Session Talking Points :

- ✓
- ✓
- ✓
- ✓
- ✓
- ✓

Next Session Date :   End Time :

Date :   Start time :   Session No :

Client Name :   Topic :

Session Talking Points :
- ✓
- ✓
- ✓
- ✓

Key Points from Previous Session :
- ✓
- ✓
- ✓
- ✓

Notes :

Extra Notes :

Client Actions :

- ✓
- ✓
- ✓
- ✓
- ✓
- ✓

Concerns :

- ✓
- ✓
- ✓

Recommendations :

- ✓
- ✓
- ✓

Overall Comments :

Next Session Talking Points :

- ✓
- ✓
- ✓
- ✓
- ✓
- ✓

Next Session Date :   End Time :

Date : _____ Start time : _____ Session No : _____
Client Name : _____ Topic : _____

Session Talking Points :
- ✓ _____
- ✓ _____
- ✓ _____
- ✓ _____

Key Points from Previous Session :
- ✓ _____
- ✓ _____
- ✓ _____
- ✓ _____

Notes : _____

Extra Notes :

Client Actions :

- ✓
- ✓
- ✓
- ✓
- ✓
- ✓

Concerns :

- ✓
- ✓
- ✓

Recommendations :

- ✓
- ✓
- ✓

Overall Comments :

Next Session Talking Points :

- ✓
- ✓
- ✓
- ✓
- ✓
- ✓

Next Session Date :   End Time :

Date :   Start time :   Session No :

Client Name :   Topic :

Session Talking Points :
- ✓
- ✓
- ✓
- ✓

Key Points from Previous Session :
- ✓
- ✓
- ✓
- ✓

Notes :

Extra Notes :

Client Actions :

- ✓
- ✓
- ✓
- ✓
- ✓
- ✓

Concerns :

- ✓
- ✓
- ✓

Recommendations :

- ✓
- ✓
- ✓

Overall Comments :

Next Session Talking Points :

- ✓
- ✓
- ✓
- ✓
- ✓
- ✓

Next Session Date :   End Time :

Date :   Start time :   Session No :

Client Name :   Topic :

Session Talking Points :
- ✓
- ✓
- ✓
- ✓

Key Points from Previous Session :
- ✓
- ✓
- ✓
- ✓

Notes :

Extra Notes :

_____
_____
_____
_____
_____

Client Actions :

- ✓ _____ ✓ _____
- ✓ _____ ✓ _____
- ✓ _____ ✓ _____

Concerns :   Recommendations :

- ✓ _____ ✓ _____
- ✓ _____ ✓ _____
- ✓ _____ ✓ _____

Overall Comments :

_____
_____
_____

Next Session Talking Points :

- ✓ _____ ✓ _____
- ✓ _____ ✓ _____
- ✓ _____ ✓ _____

Next Session Date : _____   End Time : _____

Date: Start time: Session No:

Client Name: Topic:

Session Talking Points:
- ✓
- ✓
- ✓
- ✓

Key Points from Previous Session:
- ✓
- ✓
- ✓
- ✓

Notes:

Extra Notes :

Client Actions :

- ✓
- ✓
- ✓

- ✓
- ✓
- ✓

Concerns :

- ✓
- ✓
- ✓

Recommendations :

- ✓
- ✓
- ✓

Overall Comments :

Next Session Talking Points :

- ✓
- ✓
- ✓

- ✓
- ✓
- ✓

Next Session Date : _____   End Time : _____

Date :   Start time :   Session No :

Client Name :   Topic :

Session Talking Points :
- ✓
- ✓
- ✓
- ✓

Key Points from Previous Session :
- ✓
- ✓
- ✓
- ✓

Notes :

Extra Notes :

Client Actions :
- ✓
- ✓
- ✓
- ✓
- ✓
- ✓

Concerns :
- ✓
- ✓
- ✓

Recommendations :
- ✓
- ✓
- ✓

Overall Comments :

Next Session Talking Points :
- ✓
- ✓
- ✓
- ✓
- ✓
- ✓

Next Session Date :   End Time :

Date :   Start time :   Session No :

Client Name :   Topic :

Session Talking Points :
- ✓
- ✓
- ✓
- ✓

Key Points from Previous Session :
- ✓
- ✓
- ✓
- ✓

Notes :

Extra Notes :

_____
_____
_____
_____
_____

Client Actions :

✓ _____ ✓ _____
✓ _____ ✓ _____
✓ _____ ✓ _____

Concerns :   Recommendations :

✓ _____ ✓ _____
✓ _____ ✓ _____
✓ _____ ✓ _____

Overall Comments :

_____
_____
_____

Next Session Talking Points :

✓ _____ ✓ _____
✓ _____ ✓ _____
✓ _____ ✓ _____

Next Session Date : _____   End Time : _____

Date :   Start time :   Session No :

Client Name :   Topic :

Session Talking Points :
- ✓
- ✓
- ✓
- ✓

Key Points from Previous Session :
- ✓
- ✓
- ✓
- ✓

Notes :

Extra Notes :

Client Actions :

-
-
-
-
-
-

Concerns :

-
-
-

Recommendations :

-
-
-

Overall Comments :

Next Session Talking Points :

-
-
-
-
-
-

Next Session Date : _____   End Time : _____

Date :   Start time :   Session No :

Client Name :   Topic :

Session Talking Points :
- ✓
- ✓
- ✓
- ✓

Key Points from Previous Session :
- ✓
- ✓
- ✓
- ✓

Notes :

Extra Notes :

___

Client Actions :

- ✓
- ✓
- ✓
- ✓
- ✓
- ✓

Concerns :

- ✓
- ✓
- ✓

Recommendations :

- ✓
- ✓
- ✓

Overall Comments :

___

Next Session Talking Points :

- ✓
- ✓
- ✓
- ✓
- ✓
- ✓

Next Session Date : _____ End Time : _____

Date :   Start time :   Session No :

Client Name :   Topic :

Session Talking Points :
- ✓
- ✓
- ✓
- ✓

Key Points from Previous Session :
- ✓
- ✓
- ✓
- ✓

Notes :

Extra Notes :

Client Actions :

- ✓
- ✓
- ✓

- ✓
- ✓
- ✓

Concerns :

- ✓
- ✓
- ✓

Recommendations :

- ✓
- ✓
- ✓

Overall Comments :

Next Session Talking Points :

- ✓
- ✓
- ✓

- ✓
- ✓
- ✓

Next Session Date :   End Time :

Date :   Start time :   Session No :

Client Name :   Topic :

Session Talking Points :
- ✓
- ✓
- ✓
- ✓

Key Points from Previous Session :
- ✓
- ✓
- ✓
- ✓

Notes :

Extra Notes :

Client Actions :

- ✓
- ✓
- ✓
- ✓
- ✓
- ✓

Concerns :

- ✓
- ✓
- ✓

Recommendations :

- ✓
- ✓
- ✓

Overall Comments :

Next Session Talking Points :

- ✓
- ✓
- ✓
- ✓
- ✓
- ✓

Next Session Date :   End Time :

Date : Start time : Session No :

Client Name : Topic :

Session Talking Points :
- ✓
- ✓
- ✓
- ✓

Key Points from Previous Session :
- ✓
- ✓
- ✓
- ✓

Notes :

Extra Notes :

Client Actions :
-
-
-
-
-
-

Concerns :
-
-
-

Recommendations :
-
-
-

Overall Comments :

Next Session Talking Points :
-
-
-
-
-
-

Next Session Date : _____ **End Time :** _____

Date :   Start time :   Session No :

Client Name :   Topic :

Session Talking Points :
- ✓
- ✓
- ✓
- ✓

Key Points from Previous Session :
- ✓
- ✓
- ✓
- ✓

Notes :

Extra Notes :

Client Actions :

- ✓
- ✓
- ✓
- ✓
- ✓
- ✓

Concerns :

- ✓
- ✓
- ✓

Recommendations :

- ✓
- ✓
- ✓

Overall Comments :

Next Session Talking Points :

- ✓
- ✓
- ✓
- ✓
- ✓
- ✓

Next Session Date : _____ End Time : _____

Date :　　　　　　　　Start time :　　　　　　　　Session No :

Client Name :　　　　　　　　　　　Topic :

Session Talking Points :
- ✓
- ✓
- ✓
- ✓

Key Points from Previous Session :
- ✓
- ✓
- ✓
- ✓

Notes :

Extra Notes :

Client Actions :

- ✓
- ✓
- ✓

- ✓
- ✓
- ✓

Concerns :

- ✓
- ✓
- ✓

Recommendations :

- ✓
- ✓
- ✓

Overall Comments :

Next Session Talking Points :

- ✓
- ✓
- ✓

- ✓
- ✓
- ✓

Next Session Date :   End Time :

Date :   Start time :   Session No :

Client Name :   Topic :

Session Talking Points :
- ✓
- ✓
- ✓
- ✓

Key Points from Previous Session :
- ✓
- ✓
- ✓
- ✓

Notes :

Extra Notes :

_____
_____
_____
_____
_____

Client Actions :

- ✓ _____ ✓ _____
- ✓ _____ ✓ _____
- ✓ _____ ✓ _____

Concerns :   Recommendations :

- ✓ _____ ✓ _____
- ✓ _____ ✓ _____
- ✓ _____ ✓ _____

Overall Comments :

_____
_____
_____

Next Session Talking Points :

- ✓ _____ ✓ _____
- ✓ _____ ✓ _____
- ✓ _____ ✓ _____

Next Session Date : _____ End Time : _____

Date :   Start time :   Session No :

Client Name :   Topic :

Session Talking Points :
- ✓
- ✓
- ✓
- ✓

Key Points from Previous Session :
- ✓
- ✓
- ✓
- ✓

Notes :

Extra Notes :

Client Actions :

- ✓
- ✓
- ✓

- ✓
- ✓
- ✓

Concerns :

- ✓
- ✓
- ✓

Recommendations :

- ✓
- ✓
- ✓

Overall Comments :

Next Session Talking Points :

- ✓
- ✓
- ✓

- ✓
- ✓
- ✓

Next Session Date :   End Time :

Date :   Start time :   Session No :

Client Name :   Topic :

Session Talking Points :
- ✓
- ✓
- ✓
- ✓

Key Points from Previous Session :
- ✓
- ✓
- ✓
- ✓

Notes :

Extra Notes :

Client Actions :
- ✓
- ✓
- ✓
- ✓
- ✓
- ✓

Concerns :
- ✓
- ✓
- ✓

Recommendations :
- ✓
- ✓
- ✓

Overall Comments :

Next Session Talking Points :
- ✓
- ✓
- ✓
- ✓
- ✓
- ✓

Next Session Date : _____ End Time : _____

Date :　　　　　　　　　Start time :　　　　　　　Session No :

Client Name :　　　　　　　　　　　Topic :

Session Talking Points :	Key Points from Previous Session :
✓	✓
✓	✓
✓	✓
✓	✓

Notes :

Extra Notes :

Client Actions :

- ✓
- ✓
- ✓

- ✓
- ✓
- ✓

Concerns :

- ✓
- ✓
- ✓

Recommendations :

- ✓
- ✓
- ✓

Overall Comments :

Next Session Talking Points :

- ✓
- ✓
- ✓

- ✓
- ✓
- ✓

Next Session Date :   End Time :

Date :   Start time :   Session No :

Client Name :   Topic :

Session Talking Points :
- ✓
- ✓
- ✓
- ✓

Key Points from Previous Session :
- ✓
- ✓
- ✓
- ✓

Notes :

Extra Notes :

Client Actions :

- ✓
- ✓
- ✓

- ✓
- ✓
- ✓

Concerns :

- ✓
- ✓
- ✓

Recommendations :

- ✓
- ✓
- ✓

Overall Comments :

Next Session Talking Points :

- ✓
- ✓
- ✓

- ✓
- ✓
- ✓

Next Session Date :   End Time :

Date :   Start time :   Session No :

Client Name :   Topic :

Session Talking Points :
- ✓
- ✓
- ✓
- ✓

Key Points from Previous Session :
- ✓
- ✓
- ✓
- ✓

Notes :

Extra Notes :

Client Actions :

- ✓
- ✓
- ✓

✓
✓
✓

Concerns :

- ✓
- ✓
- ✓

Recommendations :

- ✓
- ✓
- ✓

Overall Comments :

Next Session Talking Points :

- ✓
- ✓
- ✓

✓
✓
✓

Next Session Date : _____   End Time : _____

Date :   Start time :   Session No :

Client Name :   Topic :

Session Talking Points :
- ✓
- ✓
- ✓
- ✓

Key Points from Previous Session :
- ✓
- ✓
- ✓
- ✓

Notes :

Extra Notes :

Client Actions :

- ✓
- ✓
- ✓

- ✓
- ✓
- ✓

Concerns :

- ✓
- ✓
- ✓

Recommendations :

- ✓
- ✓
- ✓

Overall Comments :

Next Session Talking Points :

- ✓
- ✓
- ✓

- ✓
- ✓
- ✓

Next Session Date :   End Time :

Date :   Start time :   Session No :

Client Name :   Topic :

Session Talking Points :
- ✓
- ✓
- ✓
- ✓

Key Points from Previous Session :
- ✓
- ✓
- ✓
- ✓

Notes :

Extra Notes :

Client Actions :

-
-
-

-
-
-

Concerns :

-
-
-

Recommendations :

-
-
-

Overall Comments :

Next Session Talking Points :

-
-
-

-
-
-

Next Session Date :   End Time :

Date :   Start time :   Session No :

Client Name :   Topic :

Session Talking Points :
- ✓
- ✓
- ✓
- ✓

Key Points from Previous Session :
- ✓
- ✓
- ✓
- ✓

Notes :

Extra Notes :

Client Actions :

- ✓
- ✓
- ✓

- ✓
- ✓
- ✓

Concerns :

- ✓
- ✓
- ✓

Recommendations :

- ✓
- ✓
- ✓

Overall Comments :

Next Session Talking Points :

- ✓
- ✓
- ✓

- ✓
- ✓
- ✓

Next Session Date :   End Time :

Date :   Start time :   Session No :

Client Name :   Topic :

Session Talking Points :
- ✓
- ✓
- ✓
- ✓

Key Points from Previous Session :
- ✓
- ✓
- ✓
- ✓

Notes :

Extra Notes :

Client Actions :

- ✓
- ✓
- ✓

- ✓
- ✓
- ✓

Concerns :

- ✓
- ✓
- ✓

Recommendations :

- ✓
- ✓
- ✓

Overall Comments :

Next Session Talking Points :

- ✓
- ✓
- ✓

- ✓
- ✓
- ✓

Next Session Date : _____ End Time : _____

Date :   Start time :   Session No :

Client Name :   Topic :

Session Talking Points :
- ✓
- ✓
- ✓
- ✓

Key Points from Previous Session :
- ✓
- ✓
- ✓
- ✓

Notes :

Extra Notes :

Client Actions :

- ✓
- ✓
- ✓

- ✓
- ✓
- ✓

Concerns :

- ✓
- ✓
- ✓

Recommendations :

- ✓
- ✓
- ✓

Overall Comments :

Next Session Talking Points :

- ✓
- ✓
- ✓

- ✓
- ✓
- ✓

Next Session Date :   End Time :

Made in United States
Troutdale, OR
08/21/2023

12279772R00069